White Christmas

(Coloring Book for Kids)

Neil Masters

Copyright 2015

All Rights reserved. No part of this book may be reproduced or used in any way or form or by any means whether electronic or mechanical, this means that you cannot record or photocopy any material ideas or tips that are provided in this book.

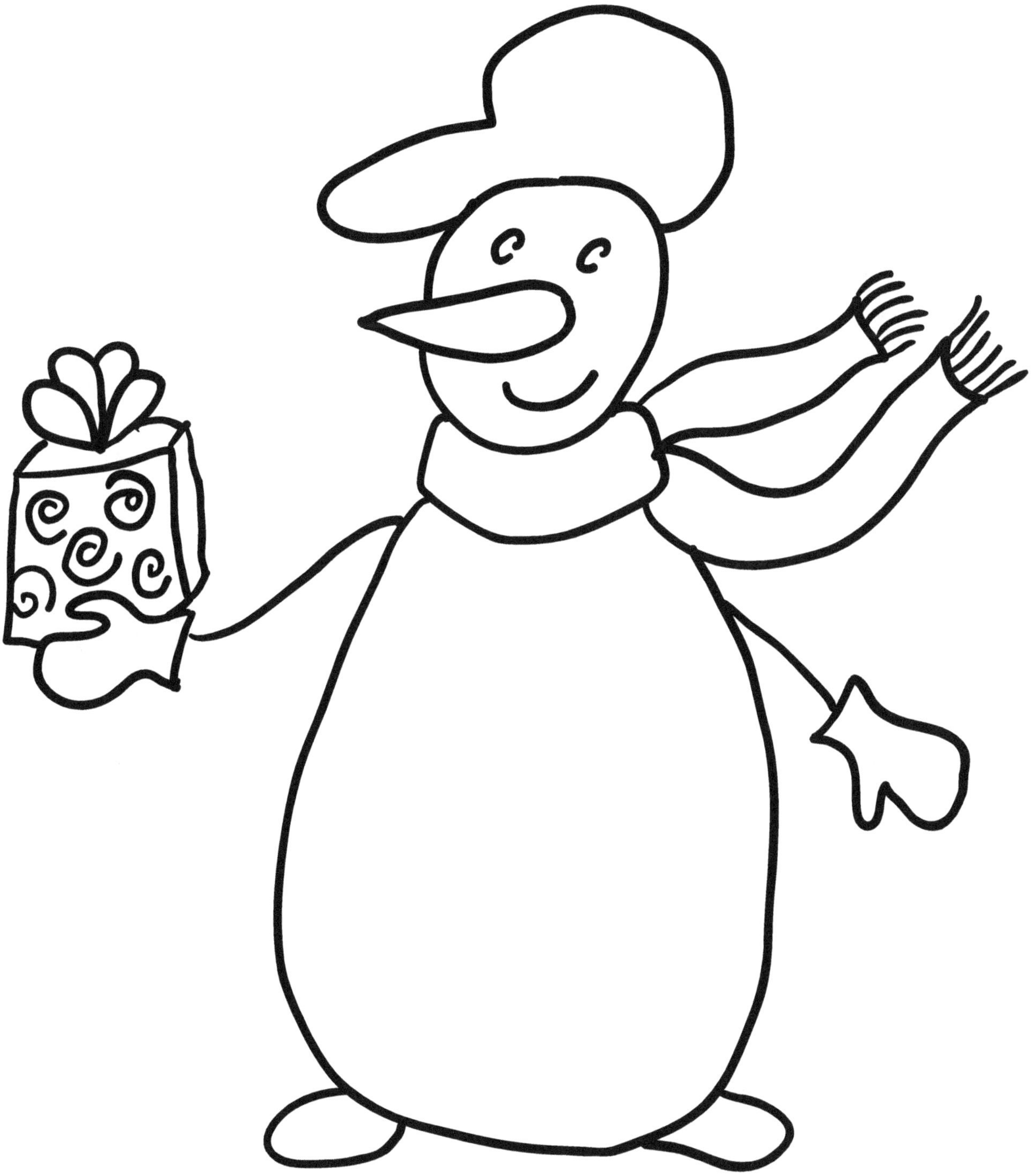

CPSIA information can be obtained
at www.ICGtesting.com
Printed in the USA
LVHW061534031220
673313LV00023B/171